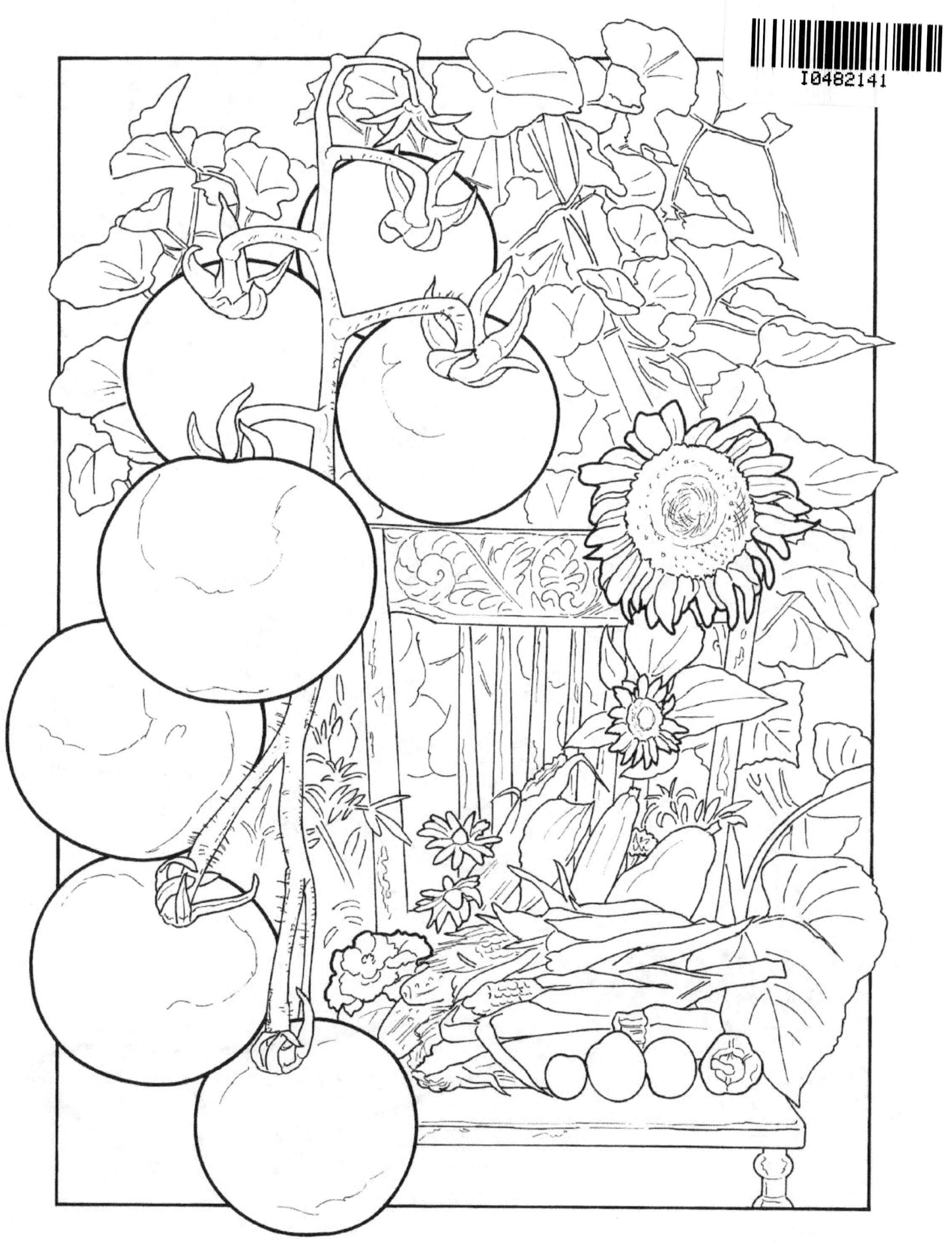

Most frogs hatch from an egg
as a tadpole and grow into a frog.

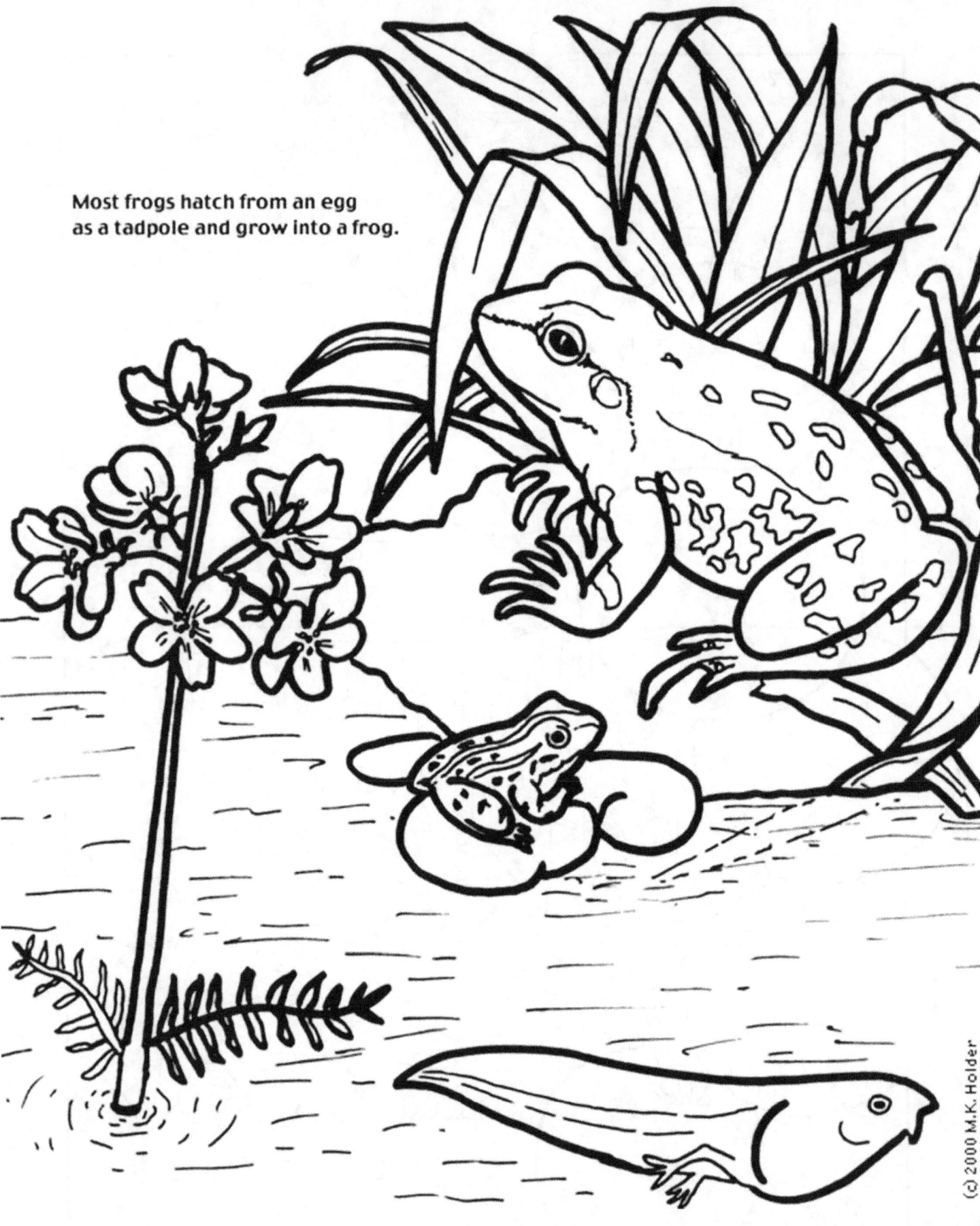

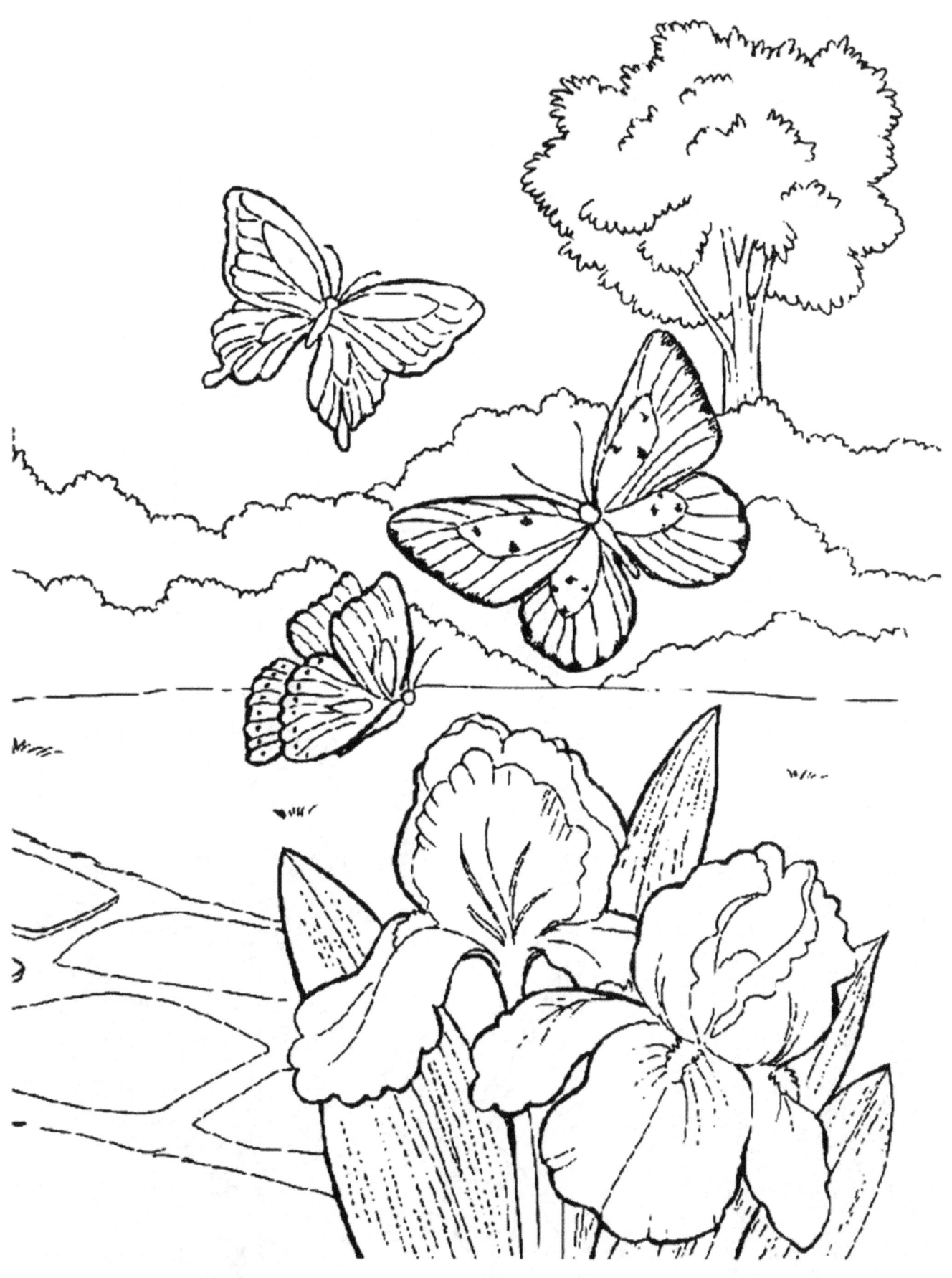

Butterflies on Iris

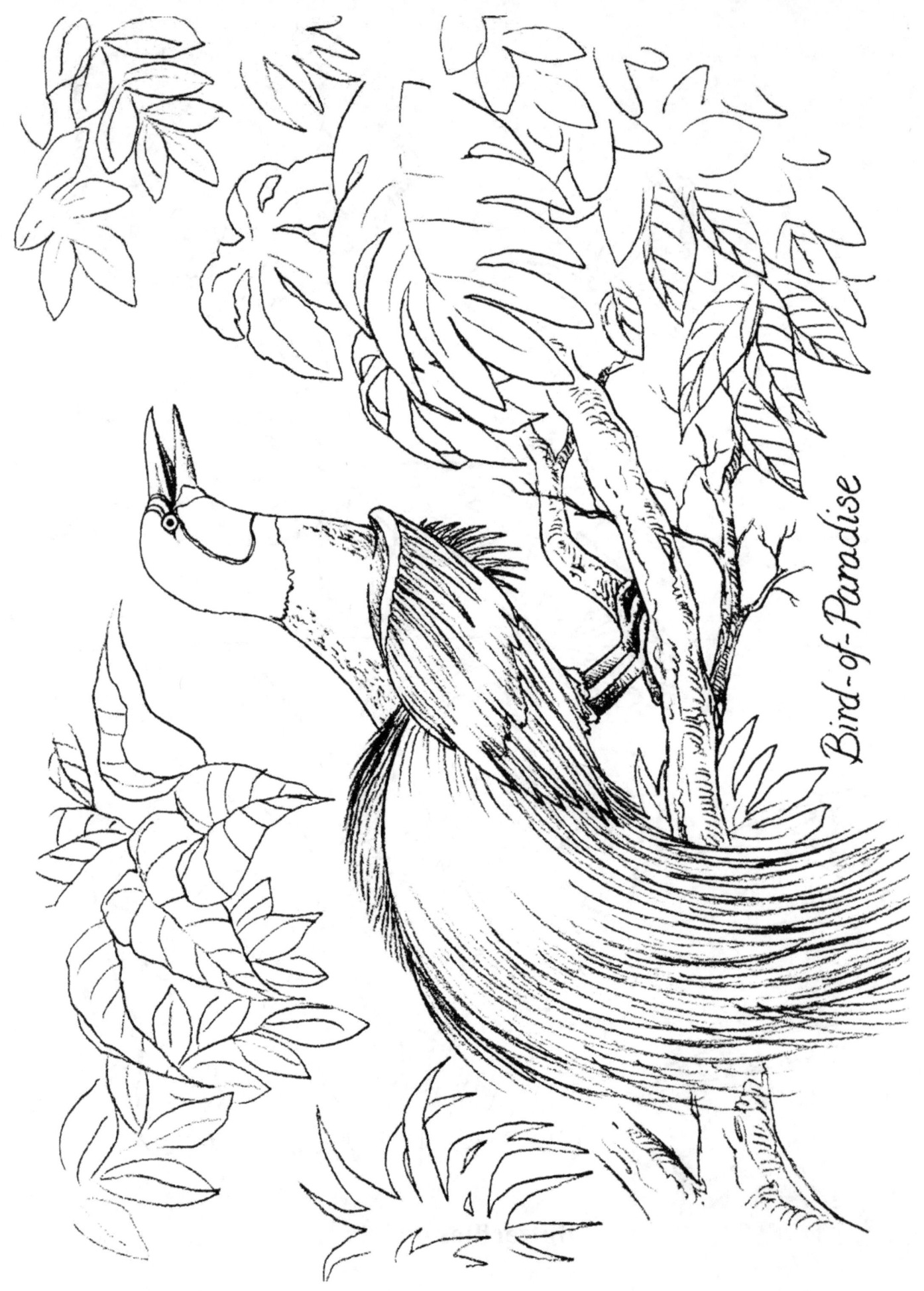

Bird-of-Paradise

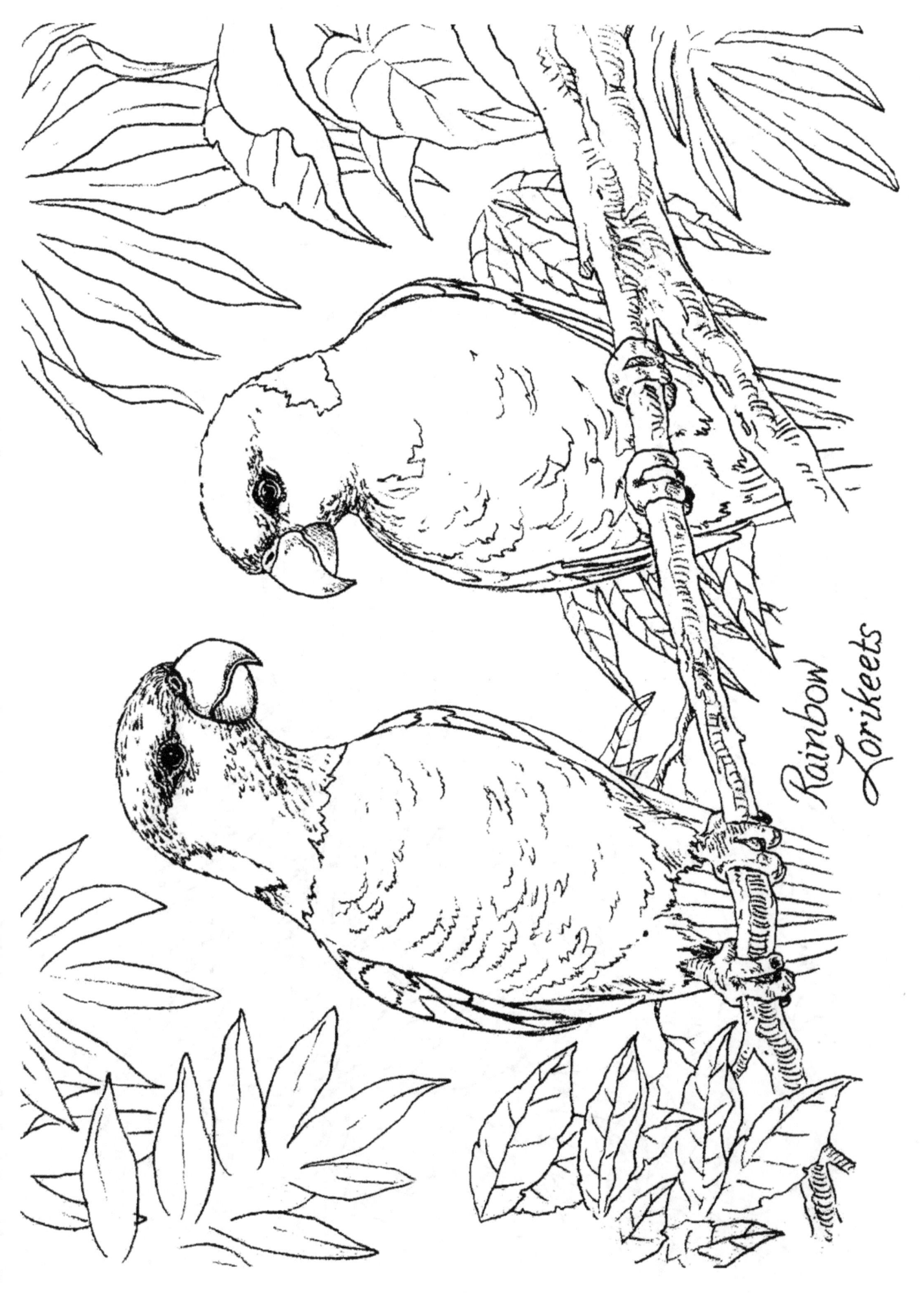

Rainbow Lorikeets

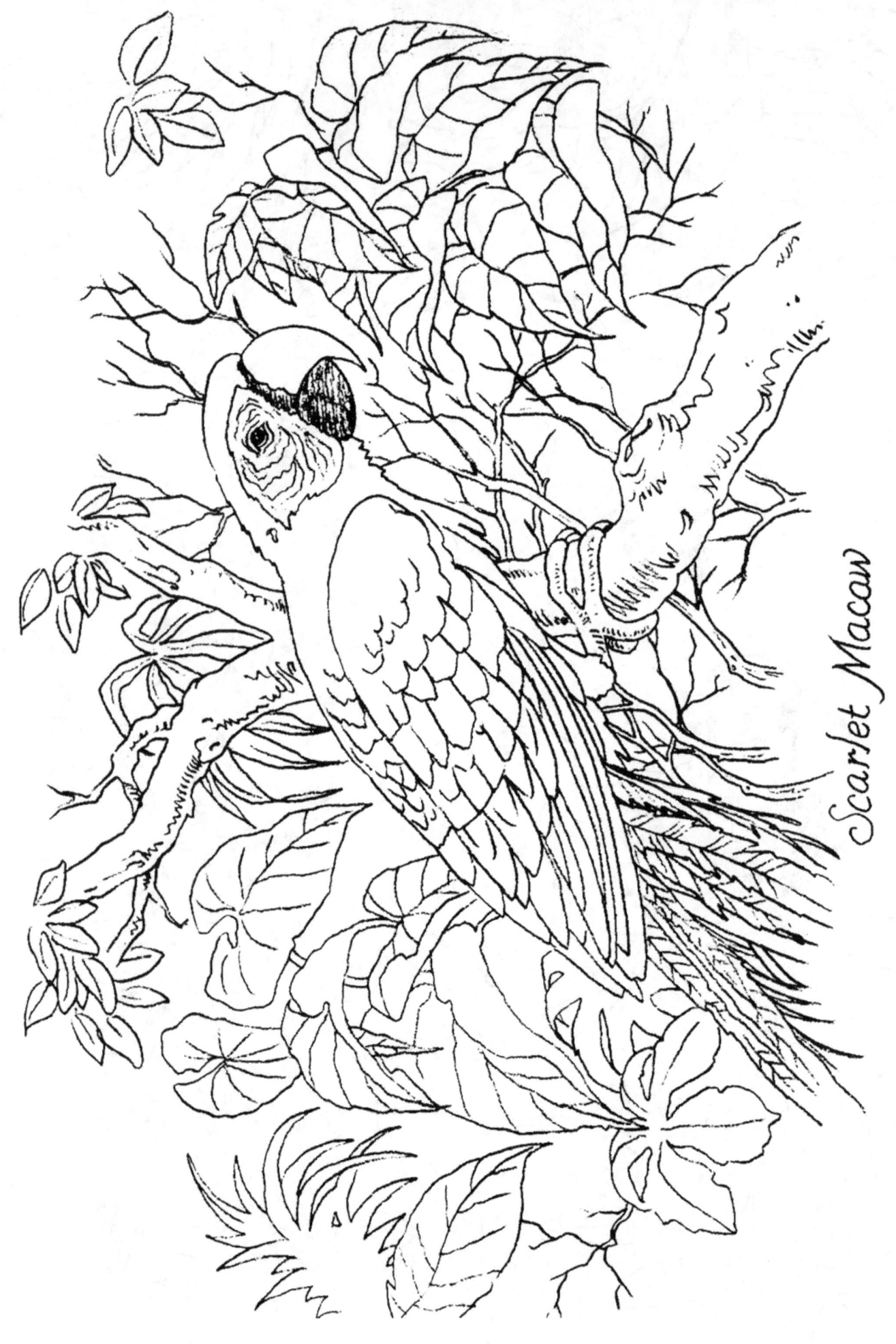

Scarlet Macaw

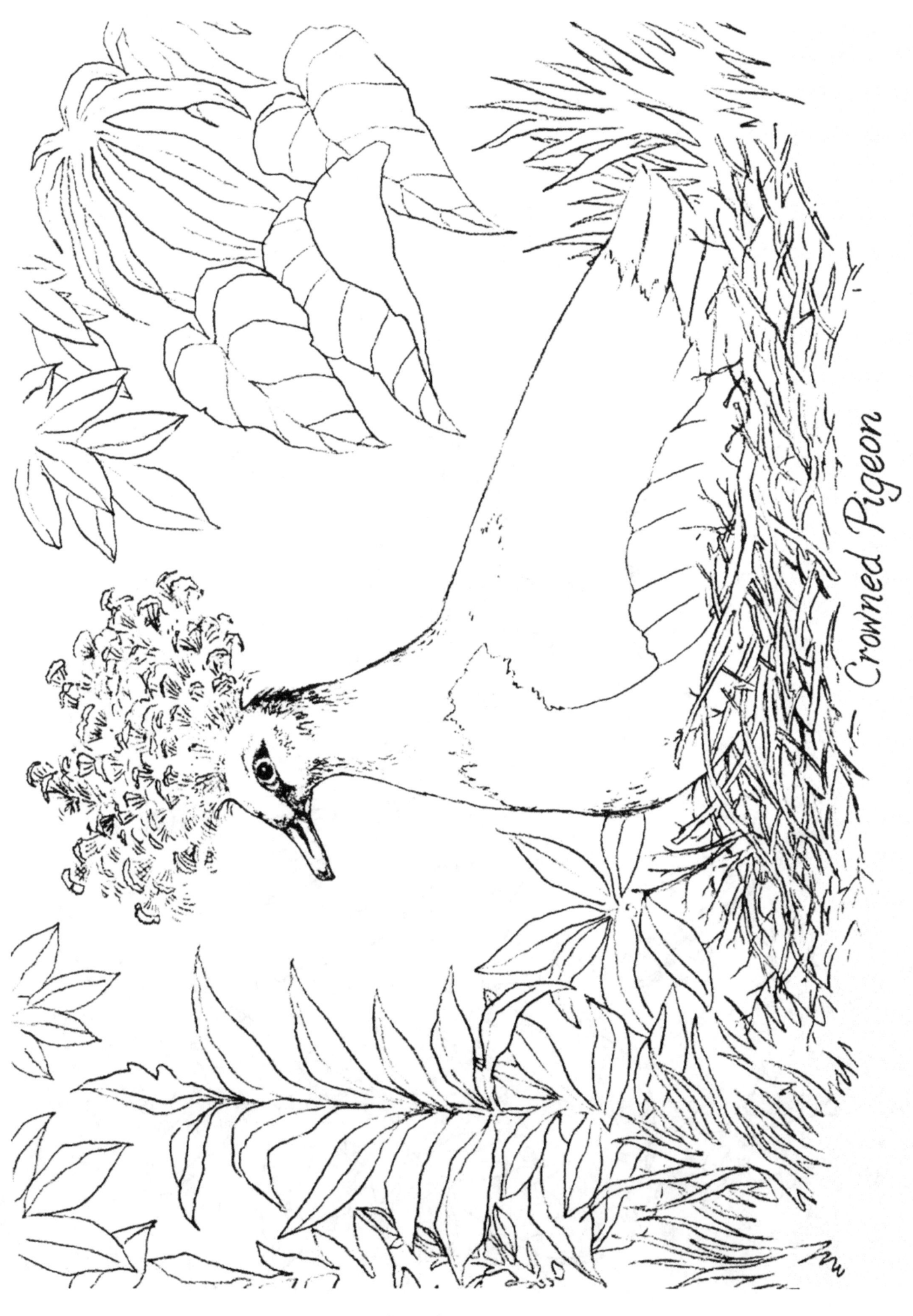

Crowned Pigeon

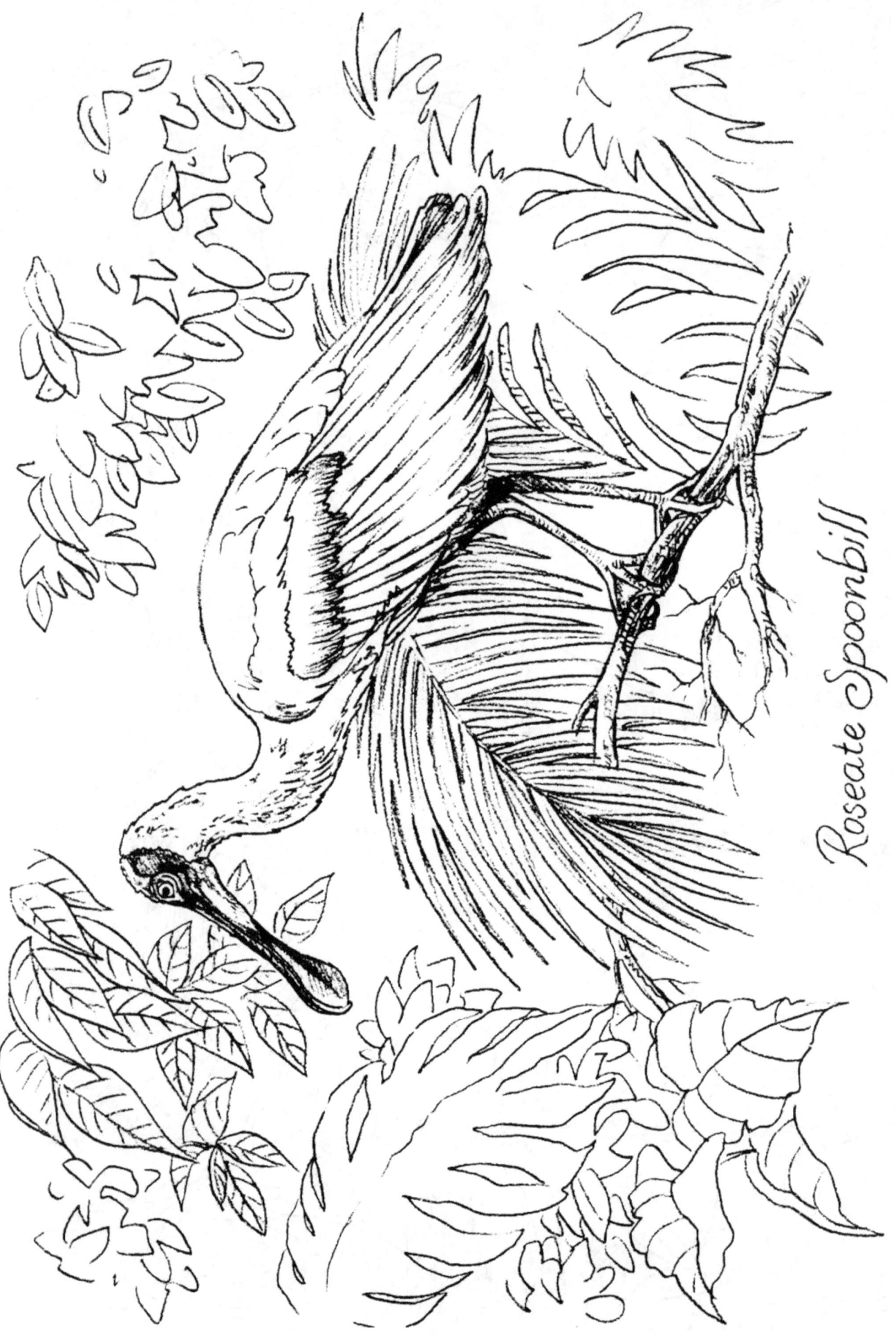

Roseate Spoonbill

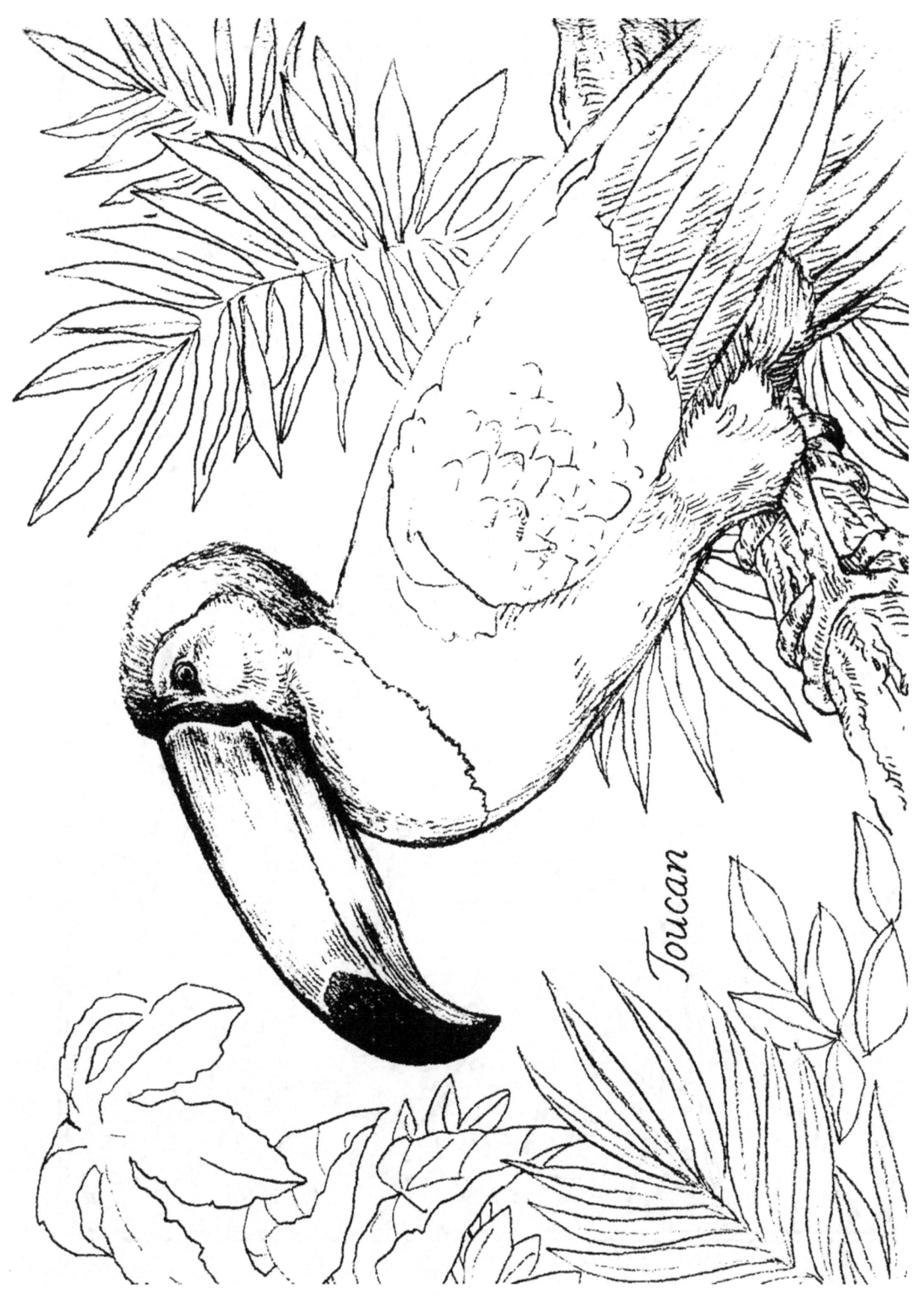

Toucan

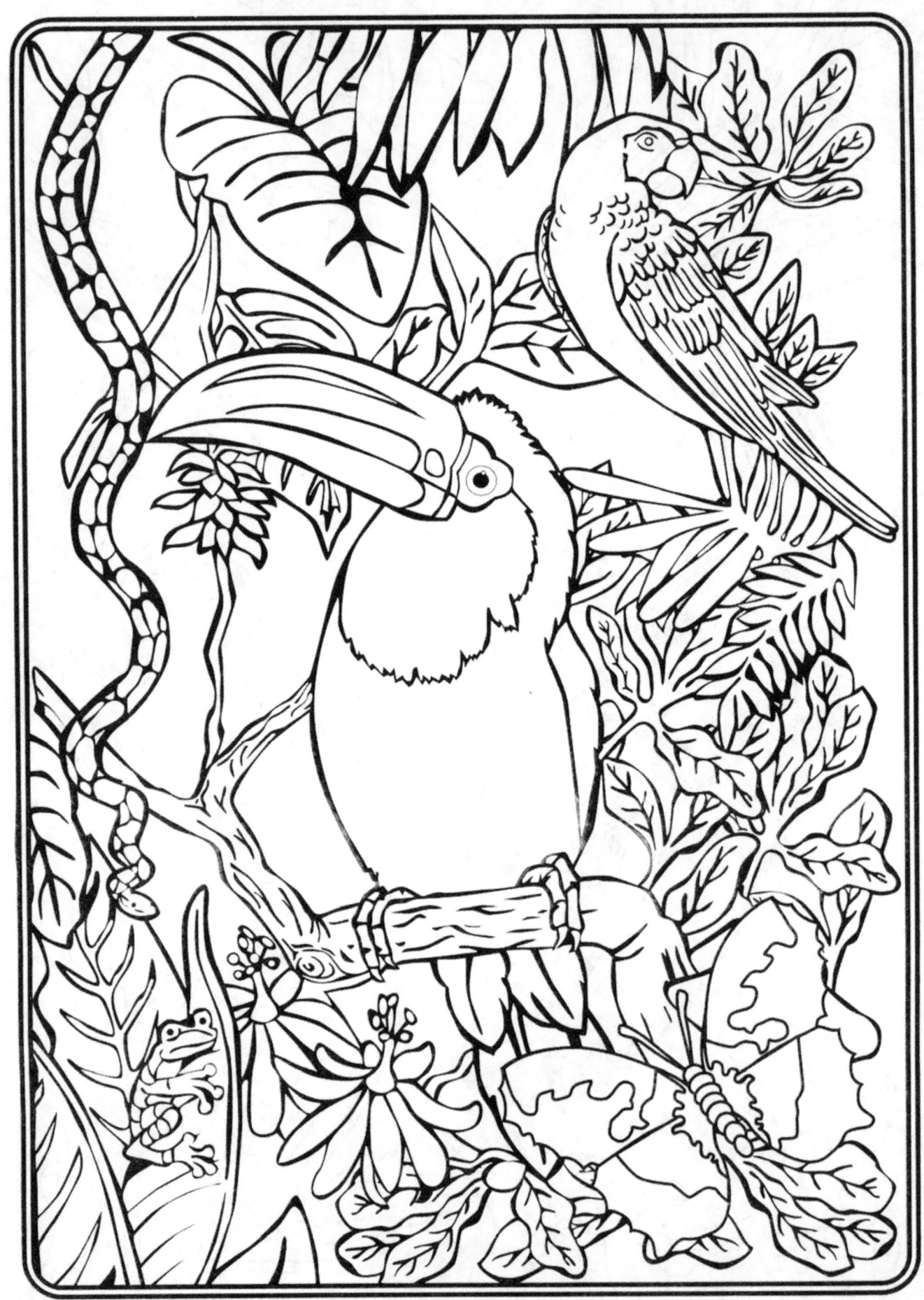

Jungle Friends

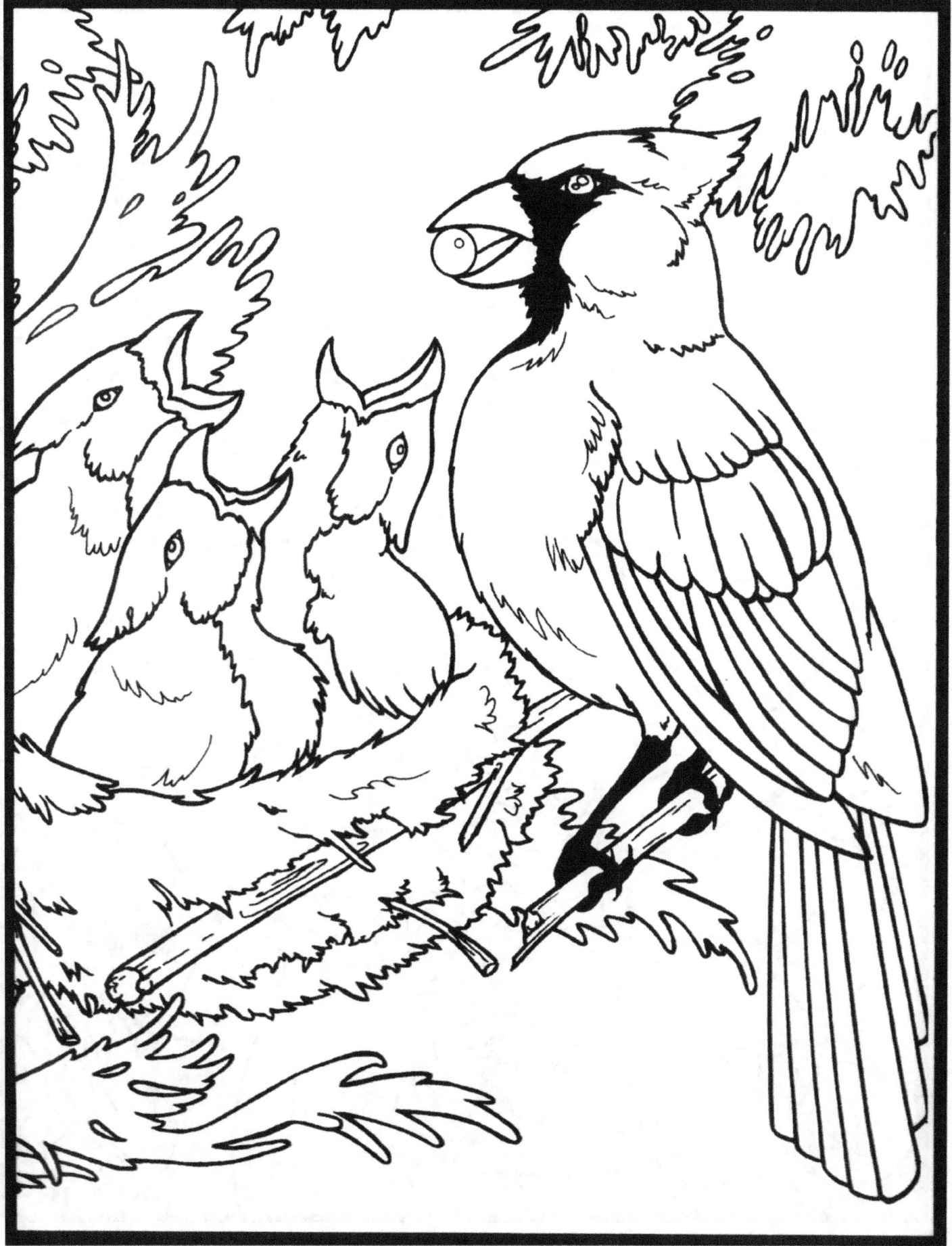

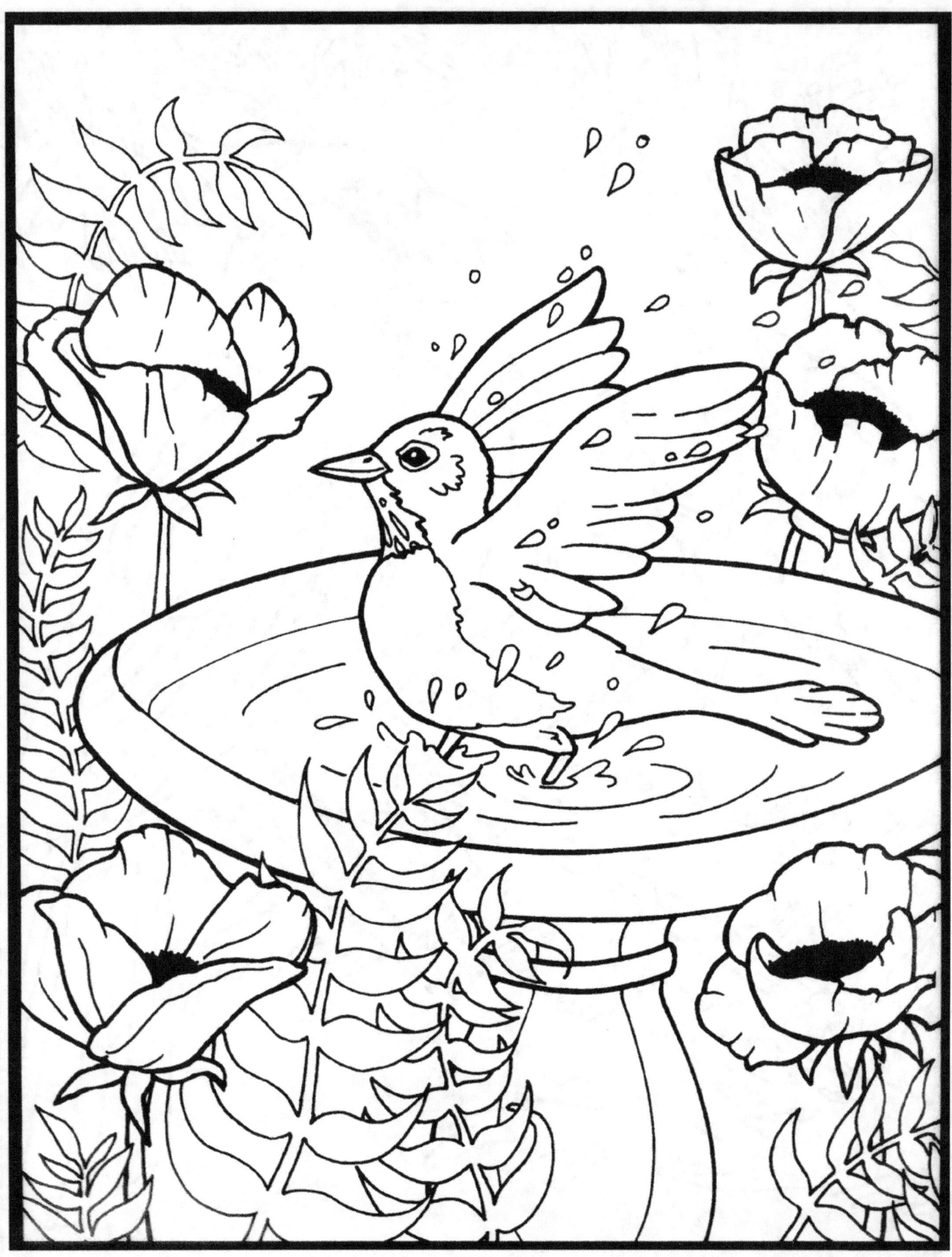

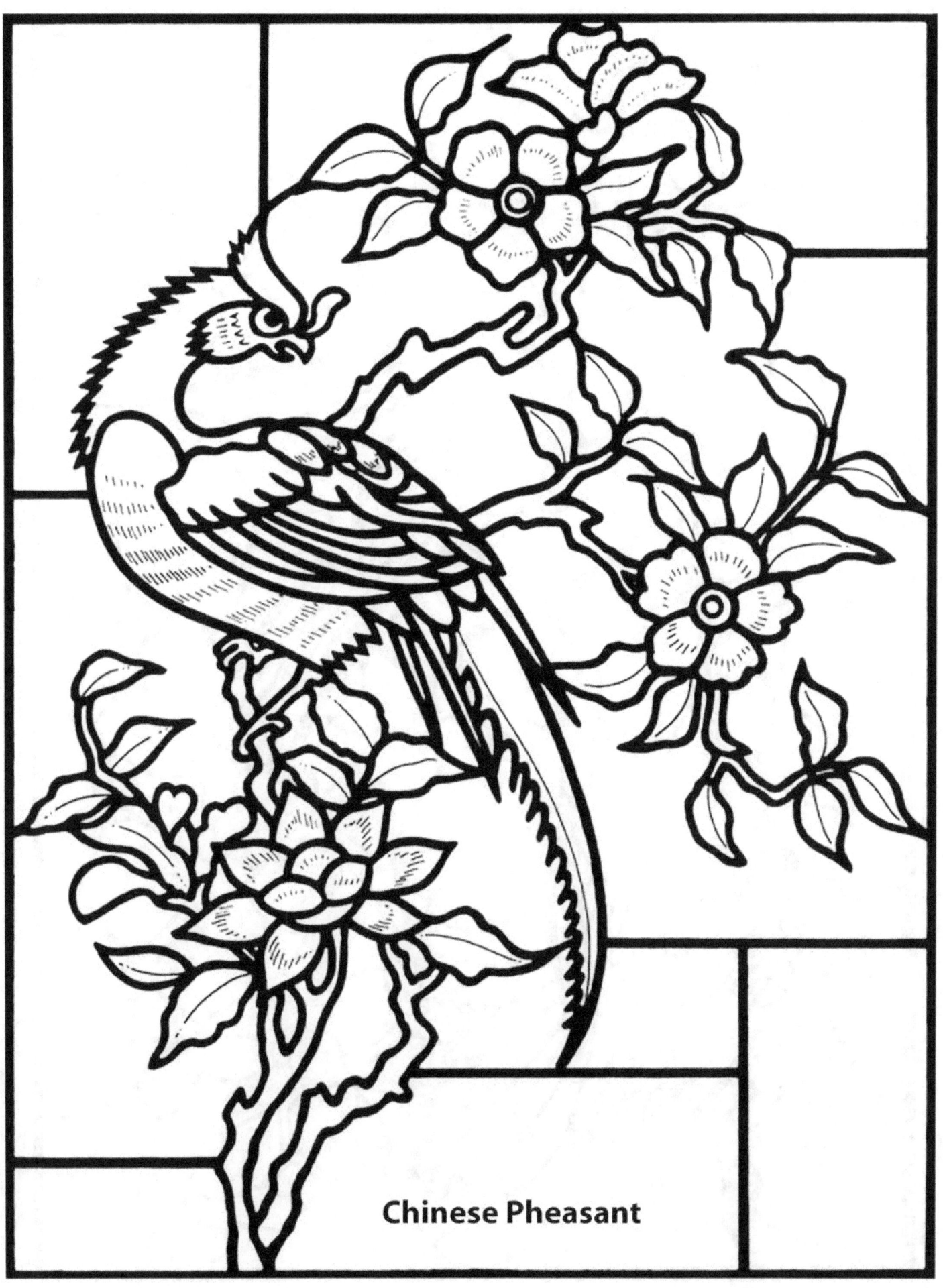

Chinese Pheasant

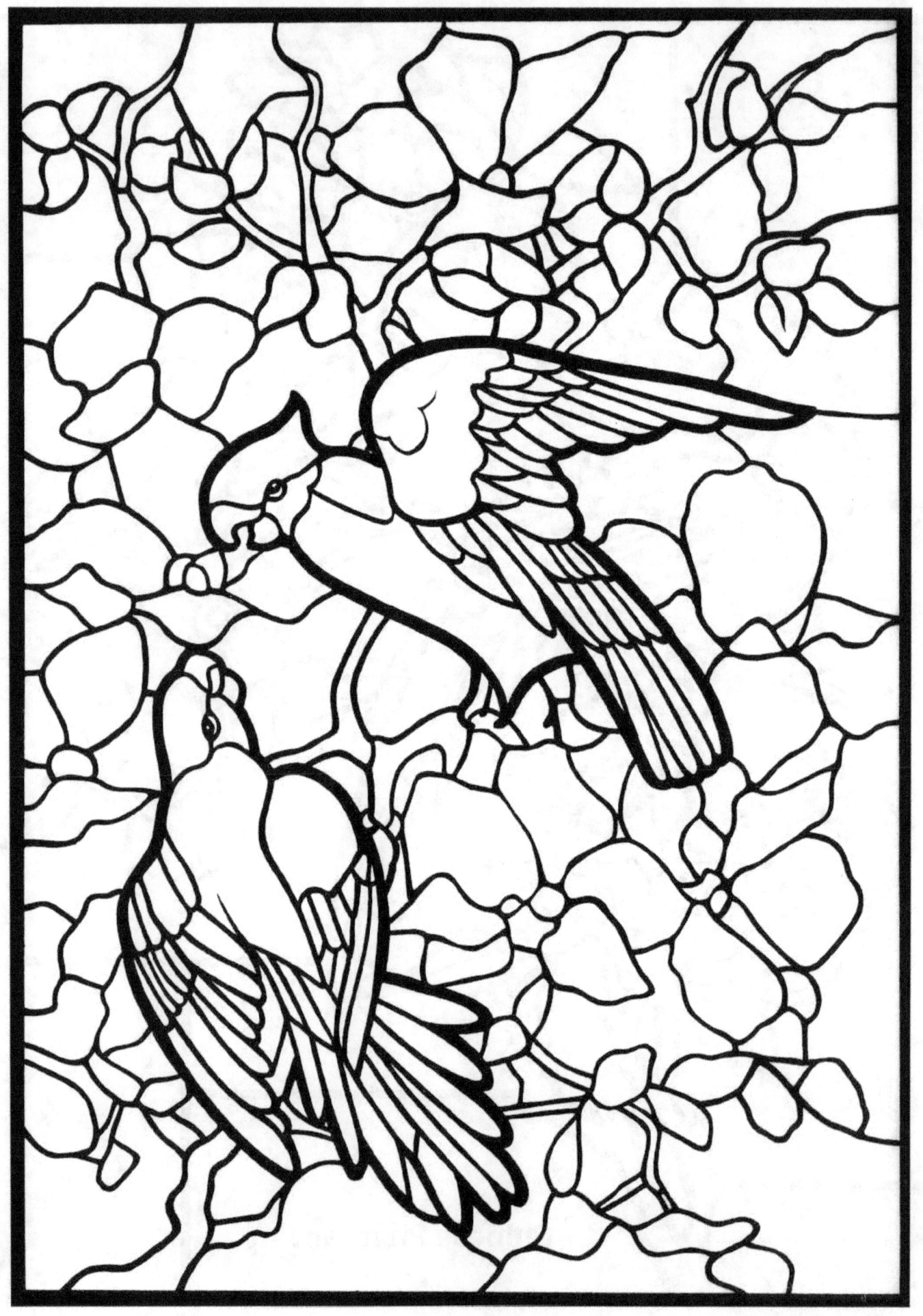

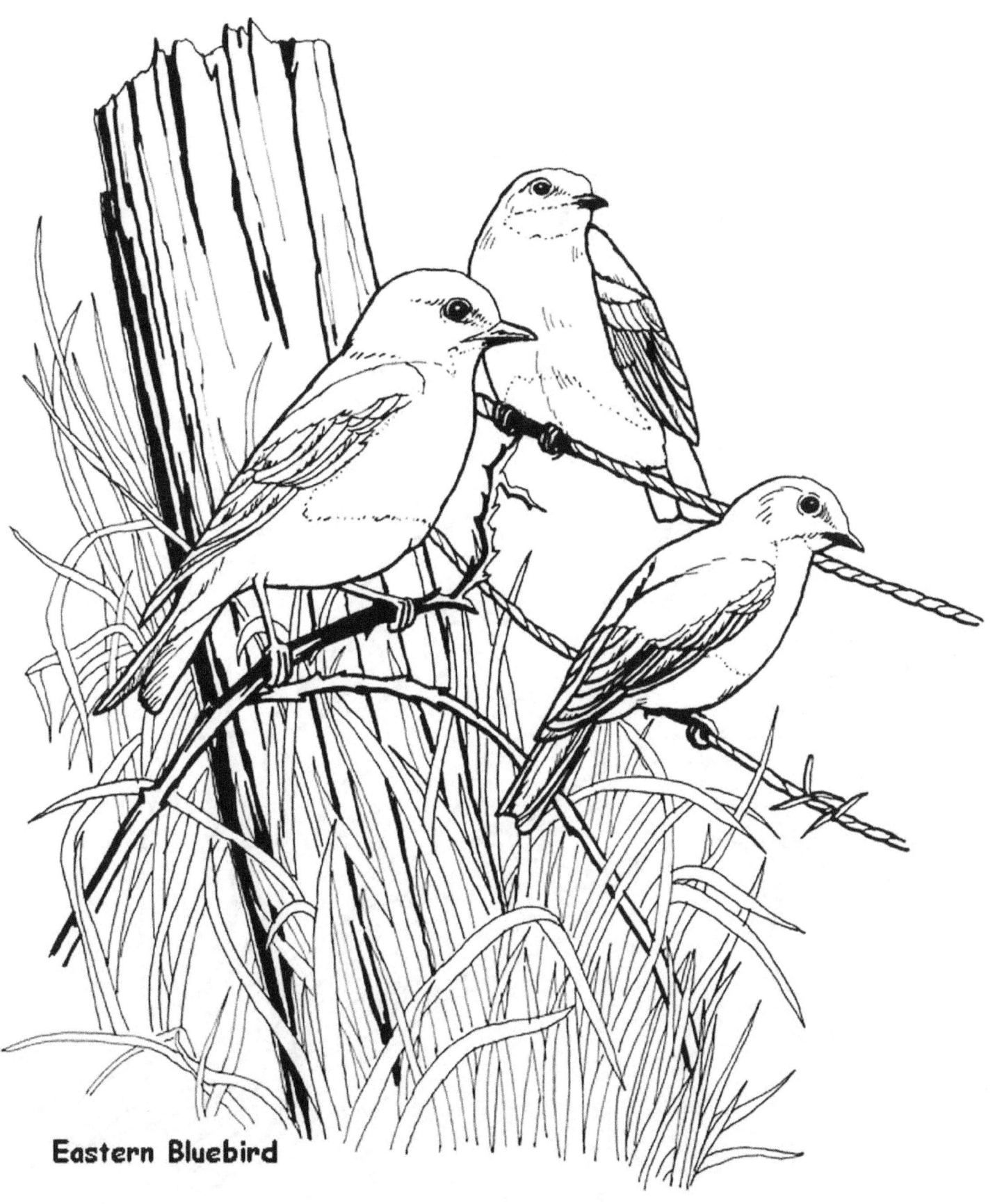

Eastern Bluebird

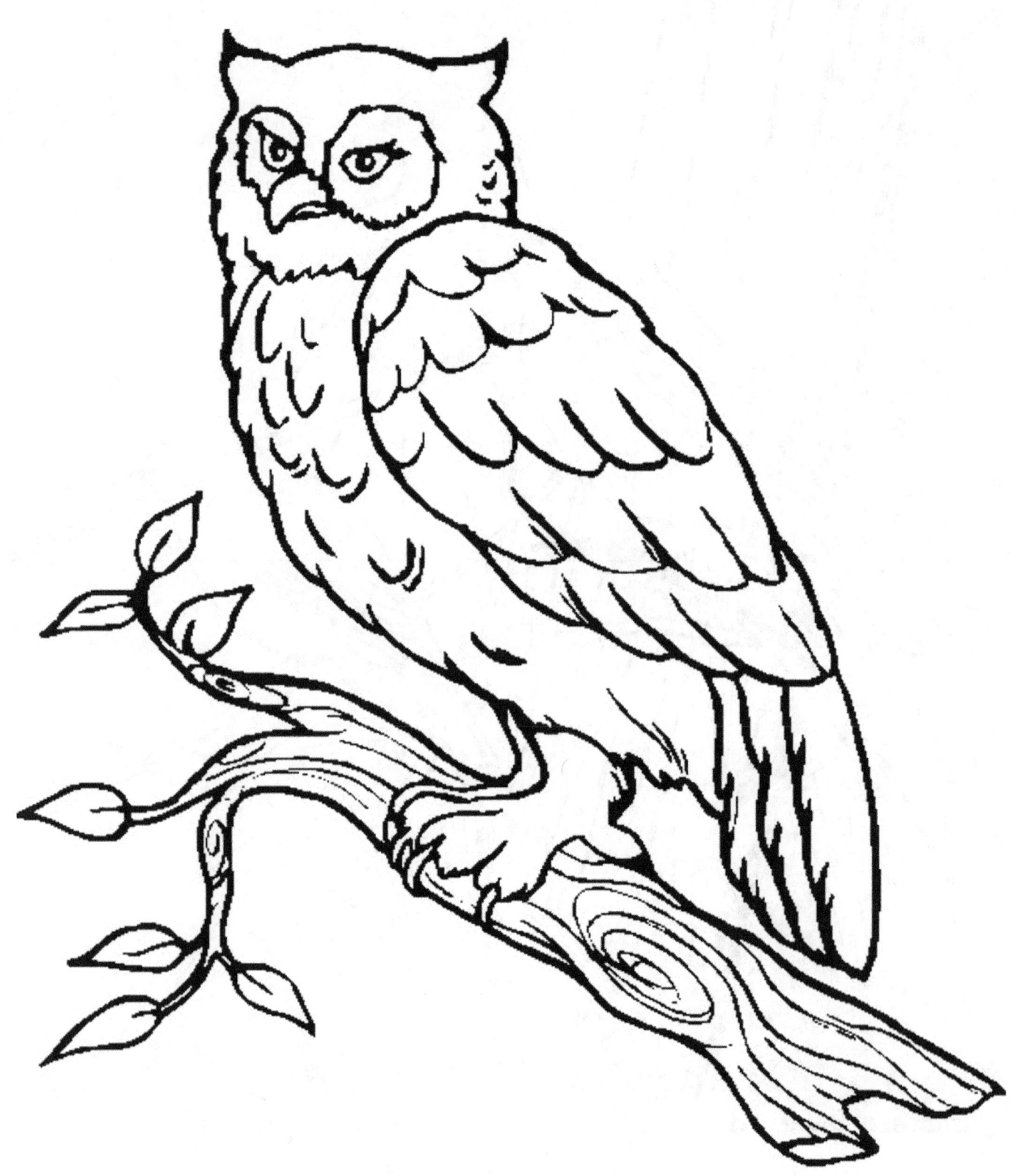

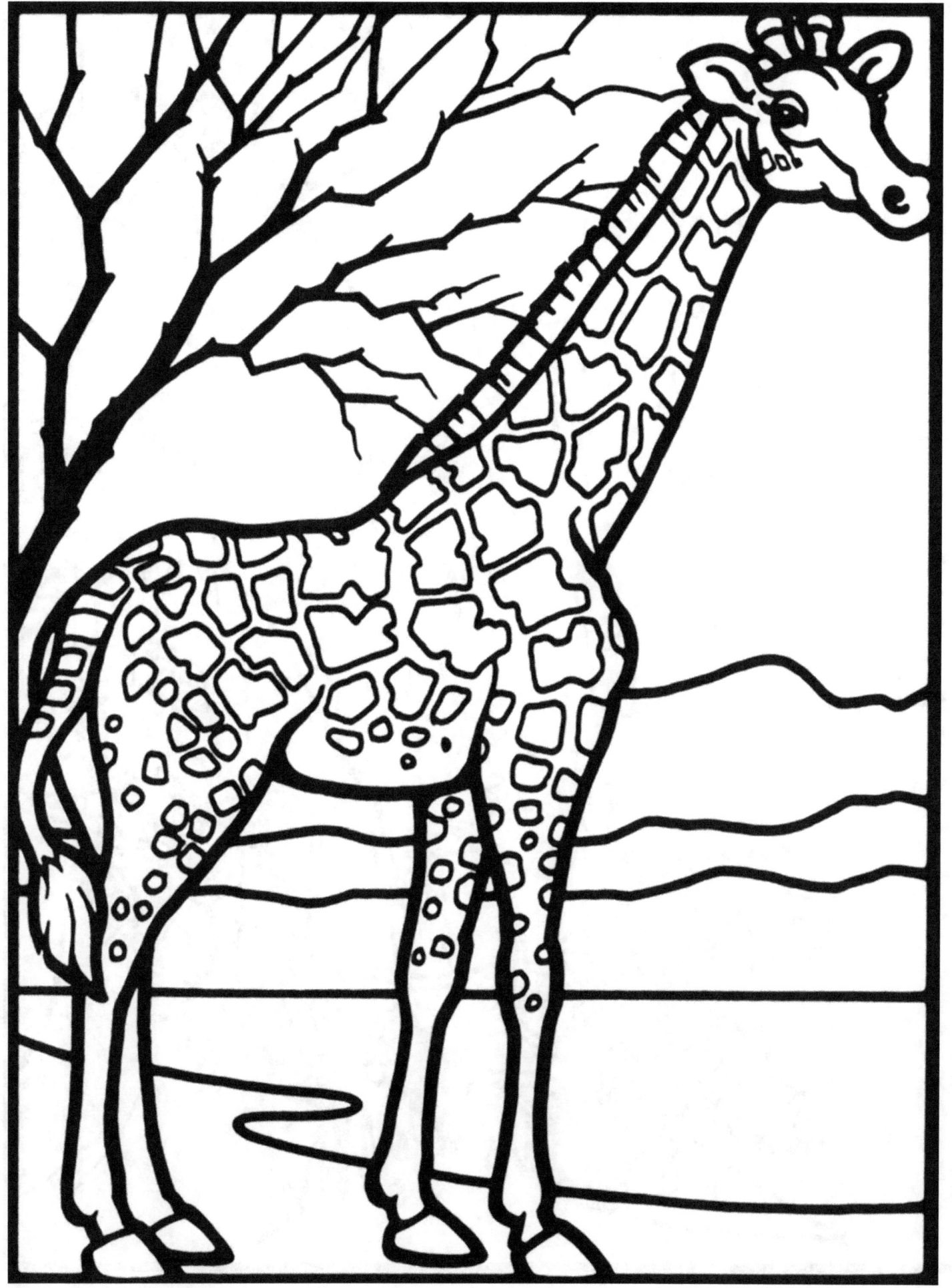

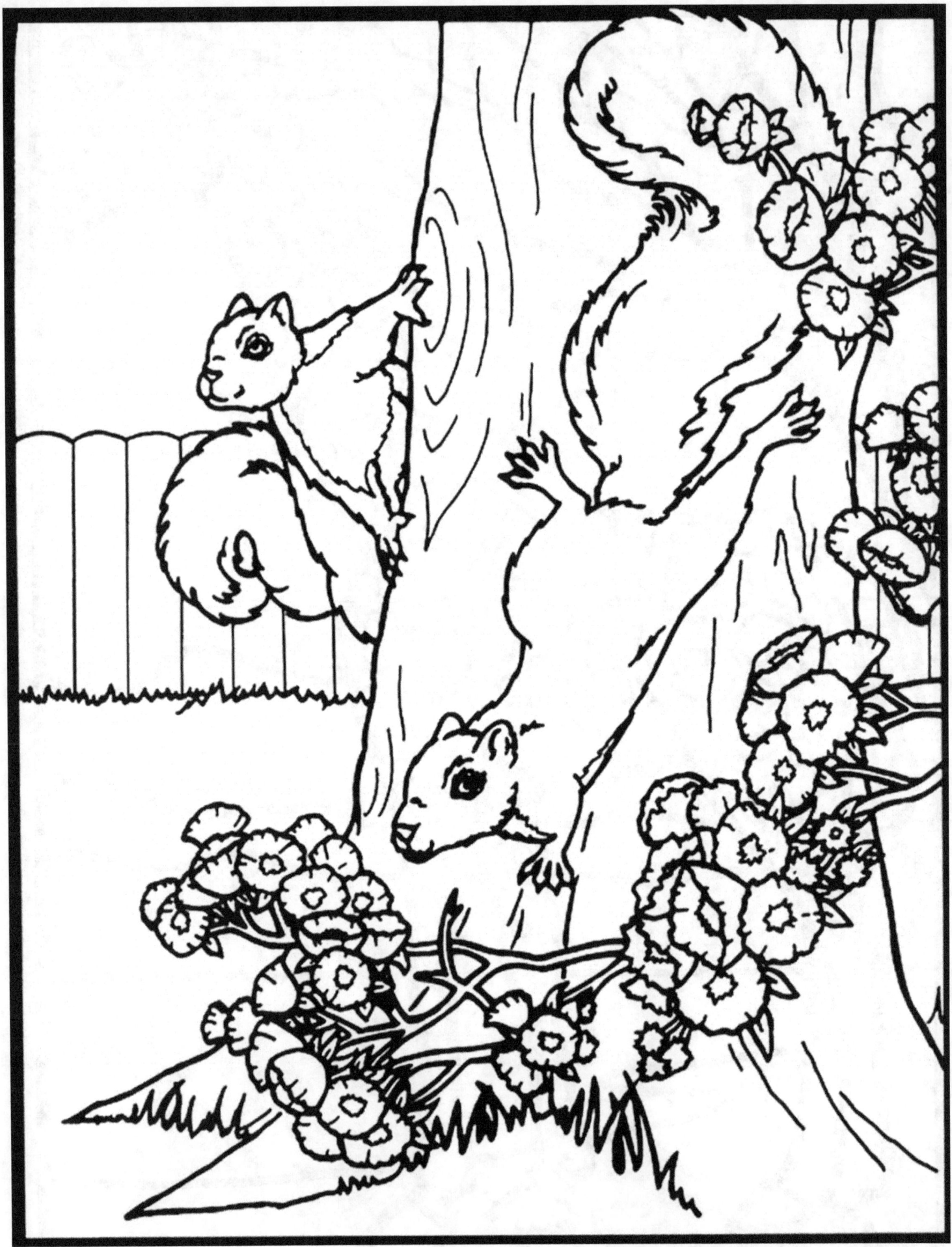

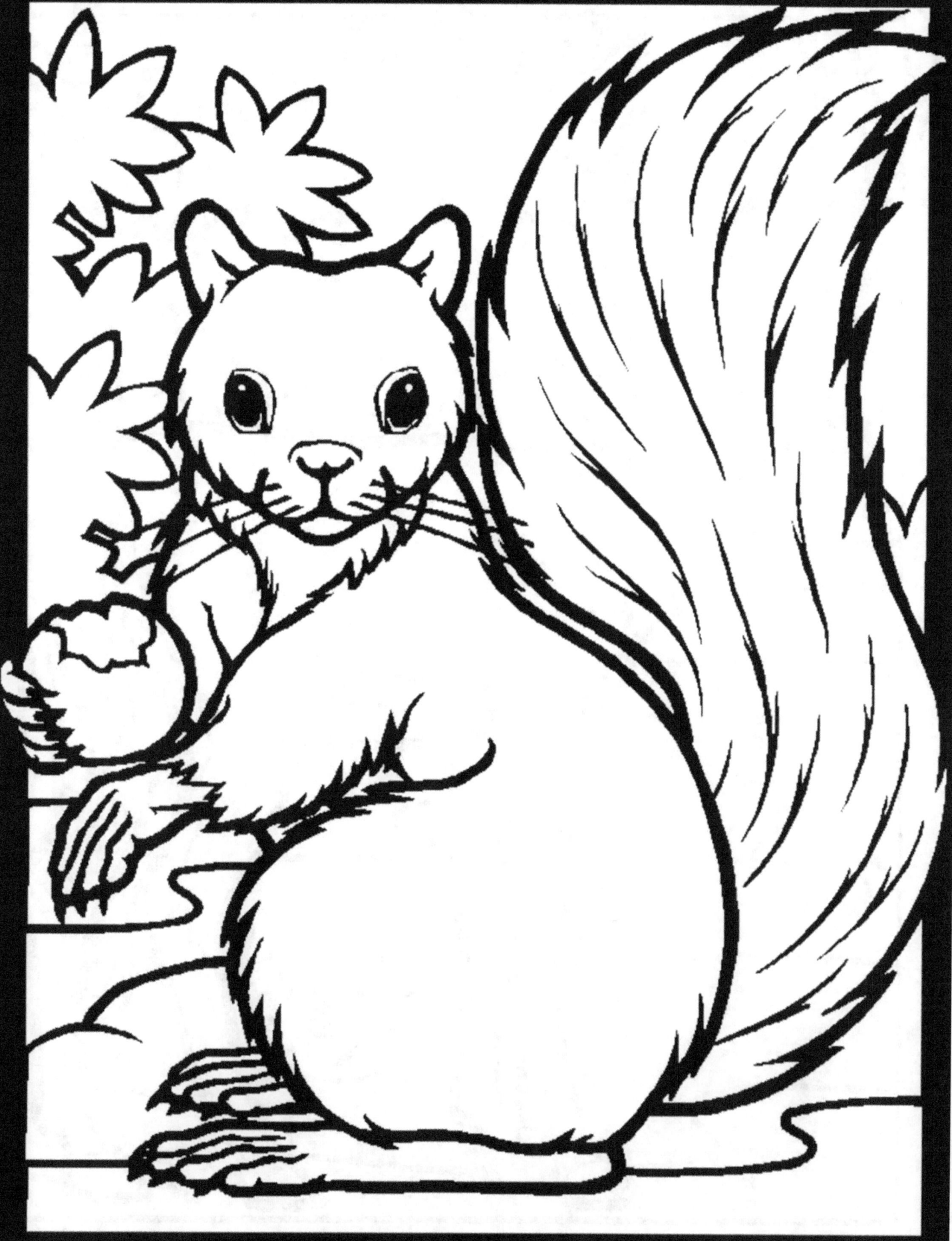

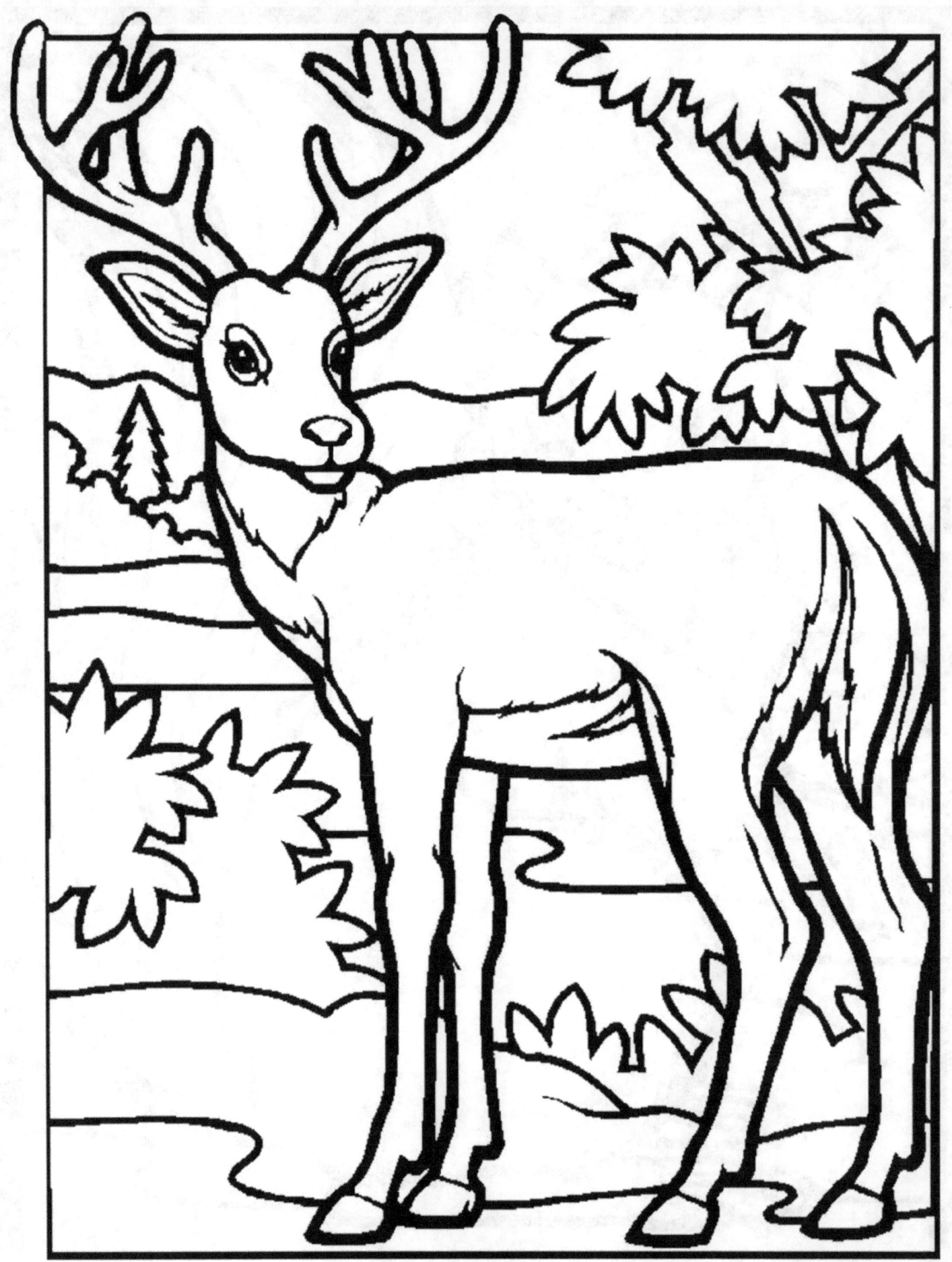

DEER

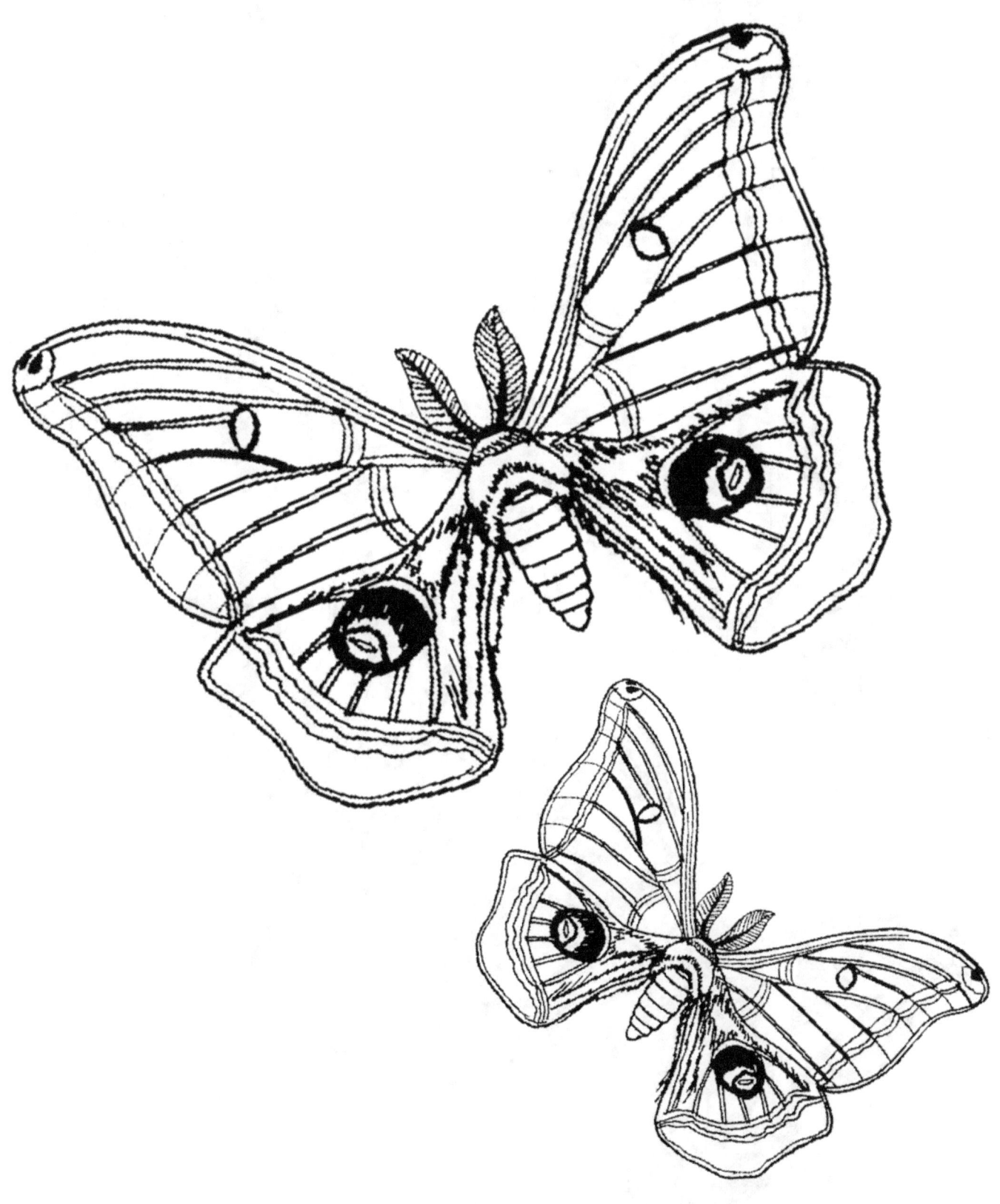

Moths

Tiger Swallowtail
Butterflies

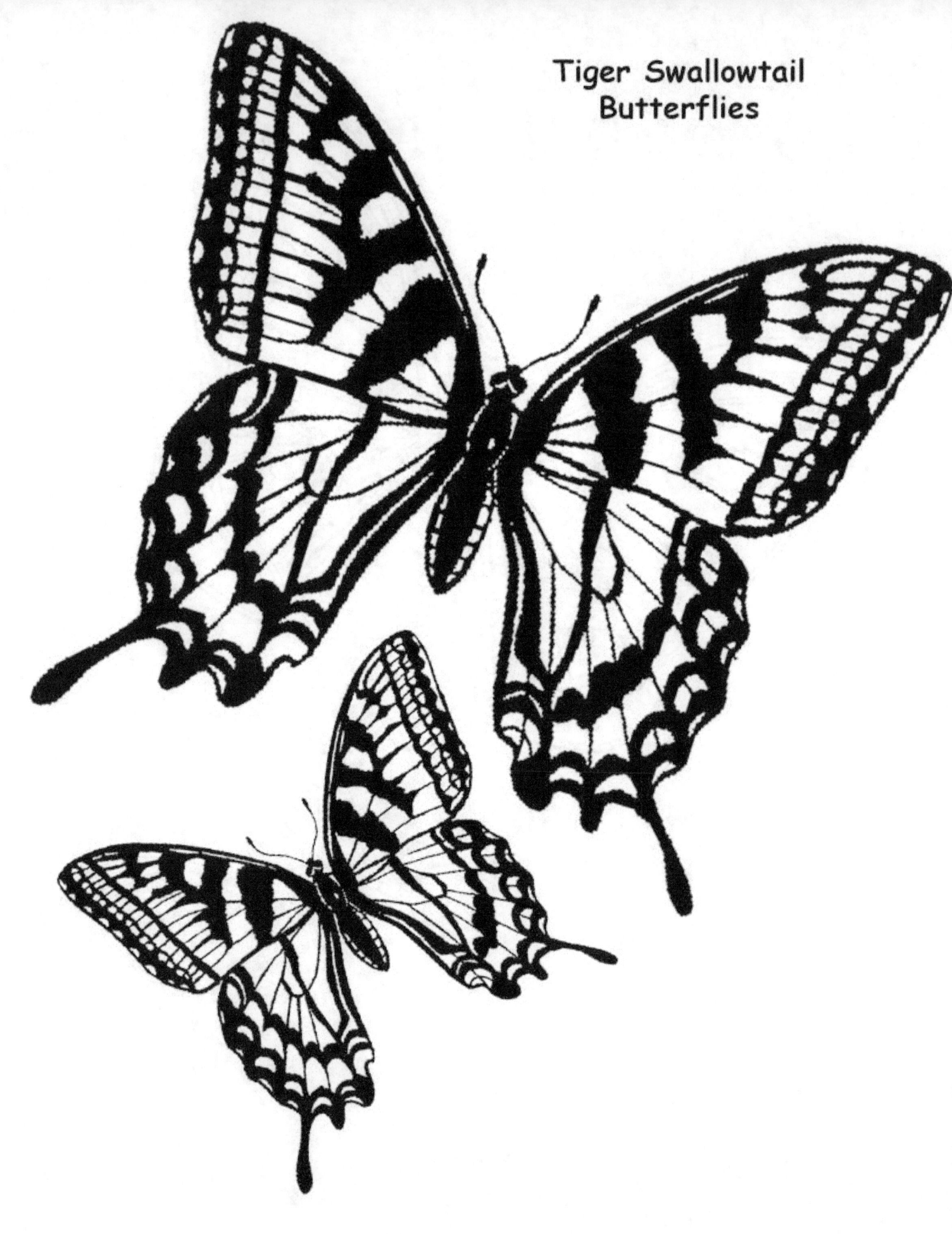

Tiger Swallowtail
Butterflies

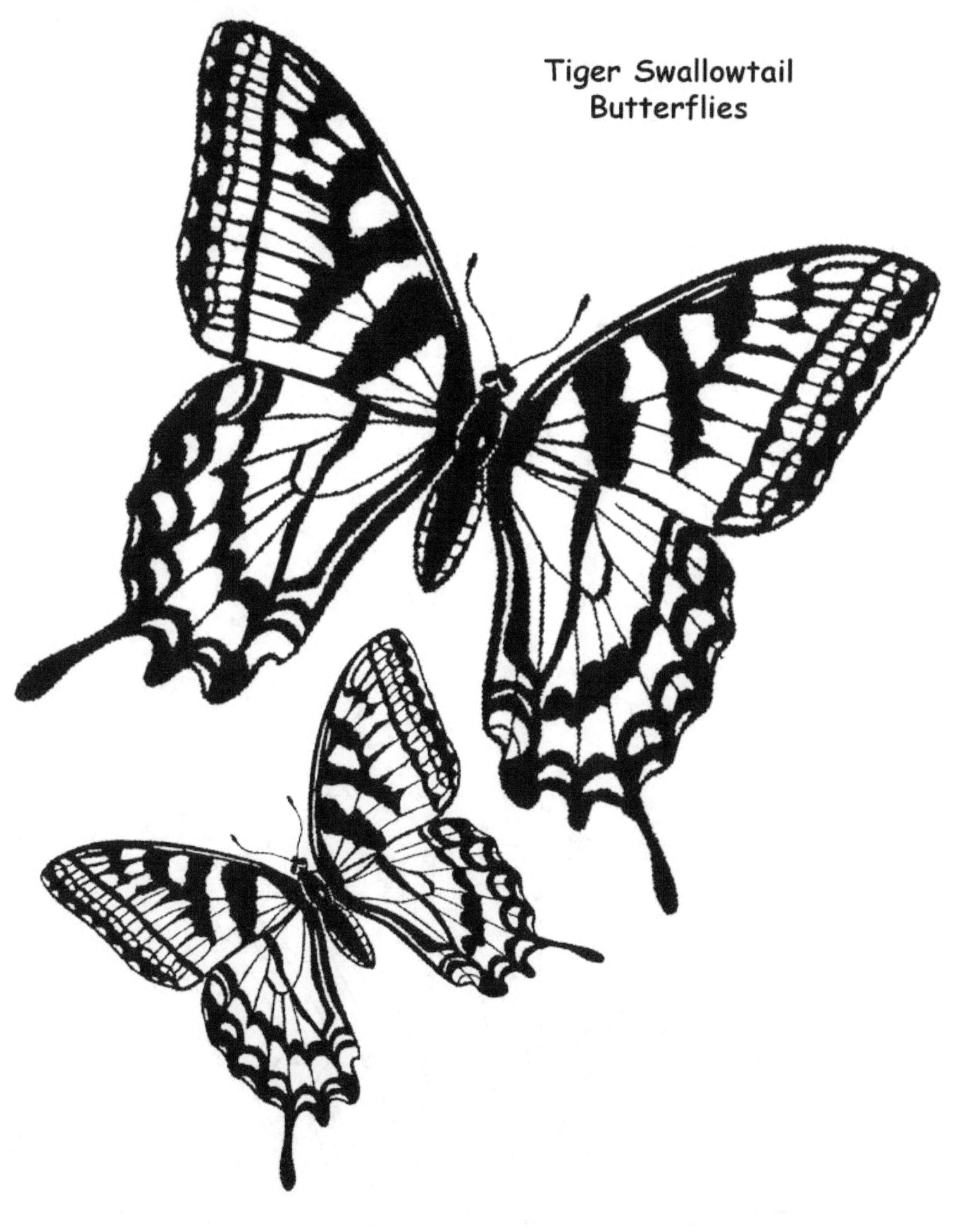

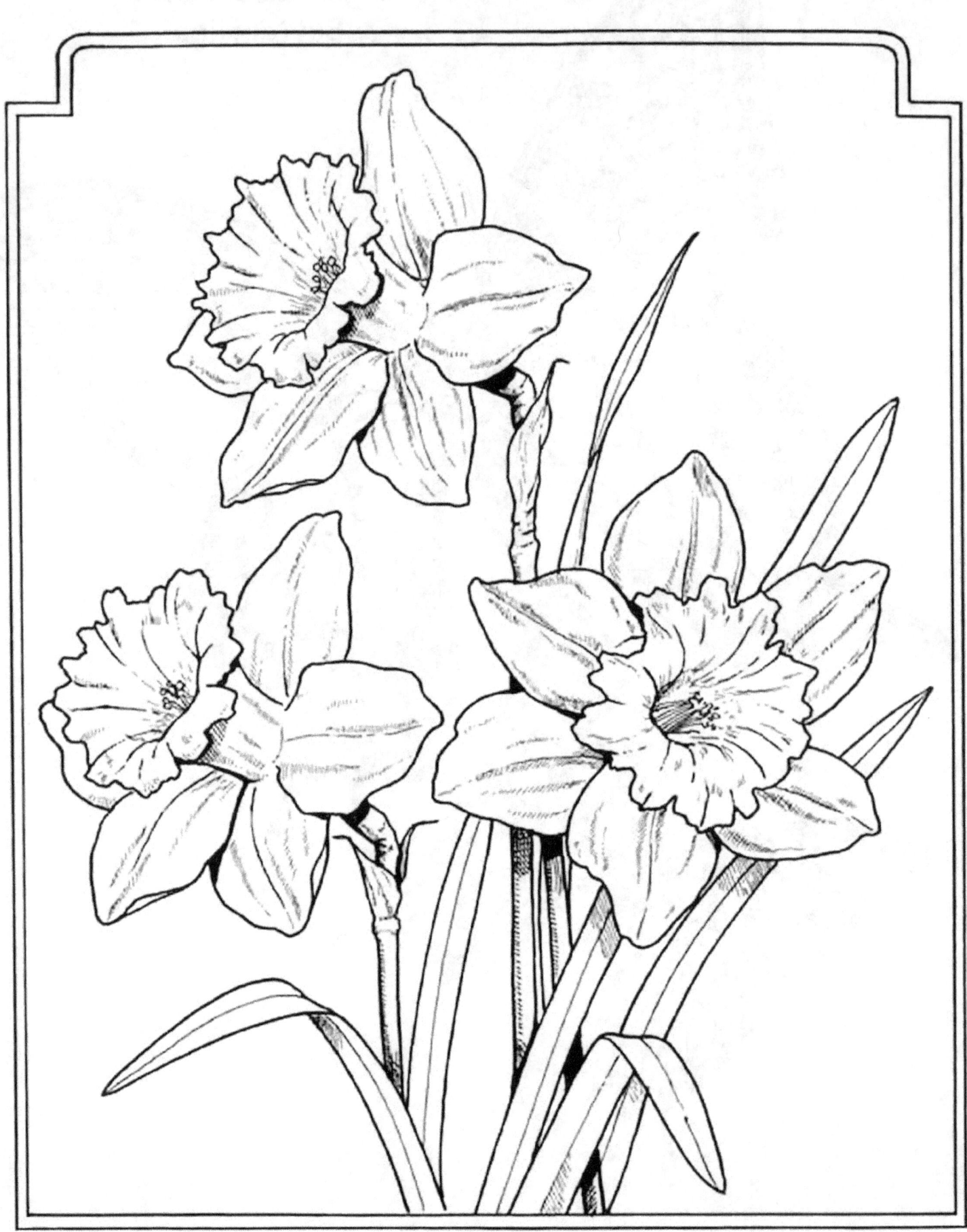

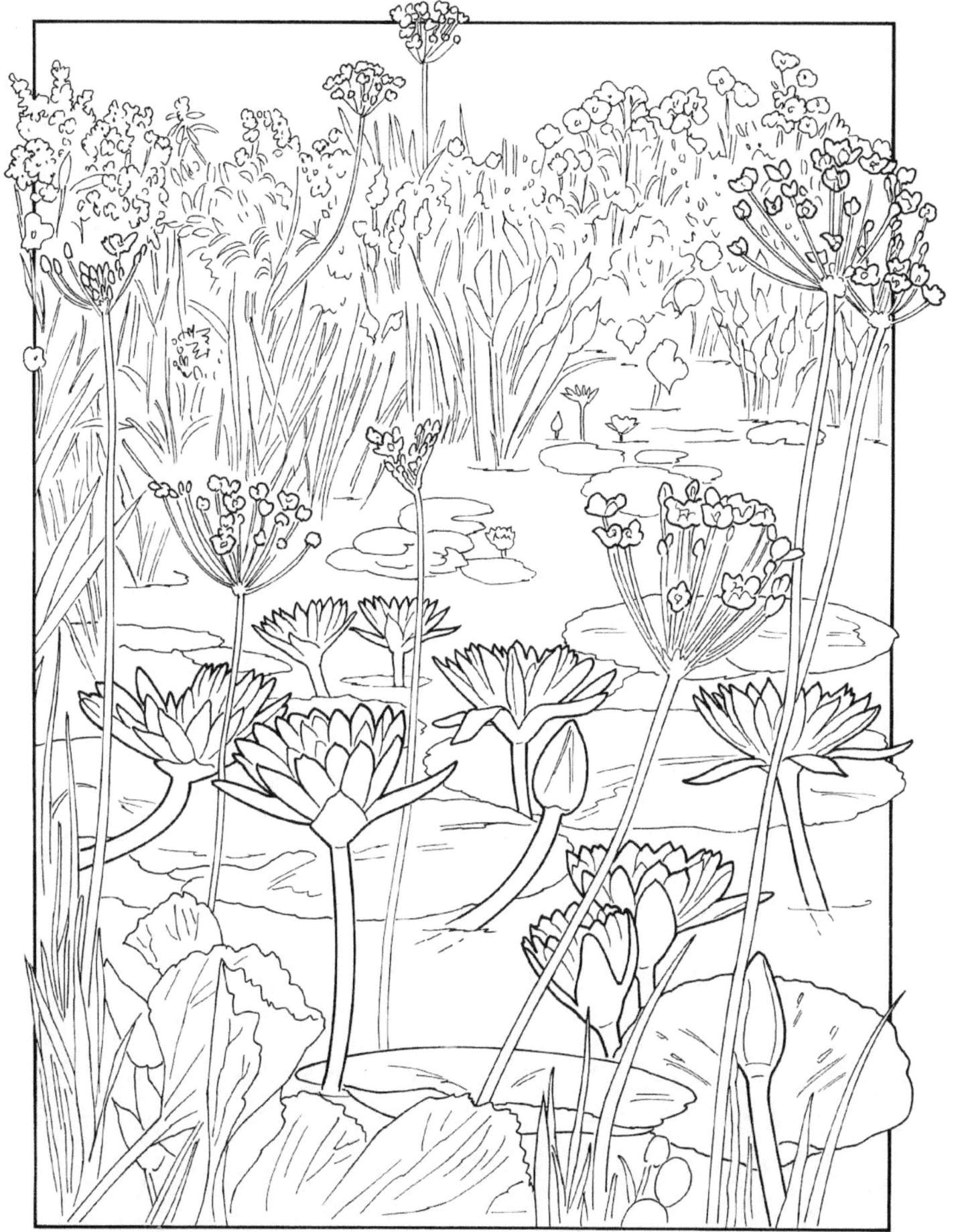